Doctors of the Church

The 33 Great Catholic Teachers

by
Fr Jerome Bertram
of the Oratory

*All booklets are published thanks to the
generous support of the members of the
Catholic Truth Society*

CATHOLIC TRUTH SOCIETY
PUBLISHERS TO THE HOLY SEE

Contents

What is a Doctor of the Church?

Among the innumerable saints honoured, venerated or forgotten in the Western Church, there is a small band of outstanding teachers, no more than thirty three in two thousand years, who have been honoured with the title of "Doctor of the Church". Since the Middle Ages it has been established that the title is conferred only by the Pope, in a public ceremony; more recently certain rules have been developed to help the Pope discern whether a particular saint is worthy of the title.

For to be a Doctor of the Church it is not enough to be holy, a worker of miracles, a shining example of Christian virtue: a Doctor is one who has something to teach, who helps the Church in the age-long process of Development of Christian Doctrine. When controversies arise, or when love grows cold, God raises up men and women with the vocation to explain disputed points of the Truth, or to call God's people back to the Way of Life, through their preaching or through their writing.

We shall understand the vocation of a Doctor of the Church best if we look at those who have already been granted the rank of Doctor, from the beginning of the Church until modern times. The title is not conferred lightly, although it is clear that some Doctors are of much greater importance than others. Some have a message that is enduring and essential for the faith of all time; others were called for particular times, and their work is done. Some have left writings that should be eagerly read by all Christians today, others are now veiled in obscurity, their writings out of print and no longer accessible. For each age, God sends the message it needs to hear; some messages need to be repeated over and over again to the end of time.

The eight original Doctors of the Church

We begin by looking at the eight teachers, three from Asia Minor, two from the North African provinces of the Roman Empire and three Europeans, who helped the Church come through the transition from a race of fugitives to become a kingdom of saints. These were the first to be acclaimed as "Doctors", and are frequently represented together in mediaeval art. Four are from the Eastern Church, four from the West, known as the Greek and Latin Doctors respectively.

The four Greek Doctors

*St Athanasius, St Basil the Great,
St Gregory of Nazianzen, St John Chrysostom*

SAINT ATHANASIUS (295-373)

Saint Athanasius towers over the turbulent fourth century, a valiant champion of the faith against the world. It was a time when the Roman Empire was at peace, and people had leisure for thought, and theological thought in particular. They cared about the truth. The disputed questions of the age were not meekly discussed in lecture rooms and studies, they were proclaimed from the housetops, argued in the streets, the matter of violent demonstrations and angry reprisals. Saint Athanasius holds the record for the number of times he was sent into exile for his teaching: he died in obscurity, but his teaching triumphed.

The question at issue can be simplified into whether Jesus is God or not. It was much more complicated than that, of course, and there were innumerable variations of teaching, some of which was clearly non-Christian, some were seen to be inadequate only with time. The whole controversy is usually known as the "Arian Crisis", and was the subject of John Henry Newman's first full-length book, *The Arians of the Fourth Century* (1833).

Christianity was now legal. Athanasius could remember the savage persecutions under Diocletian when he was a teenager, but now the new Emperor Constantine showed himself in favour of Christianity, churches were being rebuilt and religious life settled down to enjoy a period of normality. Or so they thought. In Alexandria, the chief city of Egypt and one of the most important centres of the ancient world, the bishop, aptly named Alexander, asked his clergy to give a statement of what they believed about Jesus Christ. The highly respected and scholarly senior priest Arius said that Jesus was created by God, and is the first and most important of created beings, sent to teach us how to live. He is like God, but not God by nature. The young deacon Athanasius affirmed that Jesus really is God. Alexander and his clergy felt that Athanasius was probably right, and Arius probably wrong, but were not that sure about it. So Athanasius wrote a short pamphlet, which changed the world.

The pamphlet is called *On the Incarnation*, and explains not only that Jesus really is God by nature, but also shows why he became one of us, and why it is important to grasp these essential facts. Because God is quite outside his creation, we have no means of reaching him, but are essentially other than God by nature. No matter how well we behave, we cannot reach heaven by our own efforts. But God has now entered into creation and become part of it. He is one of us, he shares our nature. This means that we are incorporated into the nature of God, and can have a share in his divinity. Athanasius put it into one crisp sentence: "He became man, so that we could become God."

This means that we are not alone in our struggle against the world, the flesh and the devil. God is truly with us, one of us. If Arius had been right, Jesus would be a good example, a teacher, someone we could try to imitate and obey, but not the essential link with the Father that we need. Athanasius taught that the whole purpose of creation itself was for God to become man, to bring mankind into union with God.

The controversy erupted throughout the world. By and large the rich and powerful, who were confident of making their own way on earth and into heaven, supported Arius, while the poor and dispossessed knew in their hearts that their Jesus is truly God. The government supported Arius, and Constantine astonished the world first by saying that really it didn't matter, then by inviting all the bishops to a council to talk about it and then, in defiance of the same council, insisting that Arius should be admitted to Communion after all. The council assembled in AD 325 at Nicaea, just across the Hellespont from the site where the Emperor was building Constantinople. The key teaching that emerged was in the familiar words, that Jesus is "true God from true God, begotten, not created, consubstantial with the Father". The word "consubstantial" represents the Greek *homoousios*, of the same nature, essence or substance as the Father. It became a battle cry during the decades that followed, for people who cared about the truth.

Although the Council of Nicaea had reached a satisfactory formula which had been accepted by all the bishops, the Emperor and his successors (who had very little understanding of what it was really all about) usually supported the "Arian" side against Athanasius, until the end of the century. The issue was simplified: instead of saying that Jesus is the most important of all creation and "like God", most settled for the easy teaching that he is just a good man, not particularly like God but a teacher worth following. In particular a Gothic preacher named Ulfilas took this opinion with him when he returned from Constantinople to evangelise his fellow Goths, so that all the Germanic tribes who were now moving into the Roman world from the north and east adopted this nicely simplified version of Christianity, and it took centuries to convert them properly with the help of St Isidore.

Athanasius began his career as a serial refugee. Now Bishop of Alexandria, he was driven into exile seven times by the Imperial supporters, on a variety of trumped-up charges, but in reality always because he

would not compromise on his teaching that Jesus is true
God. It became a proverb to talk of him as Athanasius
alone against the world, *contra mundum*. "This
extraordinary man", wrote John Henry Newman, "a
principal instrument after the Apostles by which the
sacred truths of Christianity have been conveyed and
secured to the world."

Policy in the Roman Empire was to use "internal
exile" as a punishment. That meant that Athanasius was
sent to the West, to Rome or Trier. Here he met the great
bishops of the Western church, people like St Hilary, who
had exactly the same faith as himself, and they were able
to confirm each other in their teaching. On the whole, the
bishops of the West always remained true to belief that
Jesus is God, but had not thought about it enough to be
able to hold their own in an argument. Supported and
encouraged by Athanasius, teaching was clarified in both
East and West, and as the government increasingly sent
loyal Catholics into internal exile they continually met
each other and confirmed each other in the faith as they
journeyed between East and West, like St Athanasius and
St Hilary.

But in the meantime, it seemed the government line
was winning. A series of local councils were called, at
which compromise formulas were produced, and most of
the bishops, particularly in the East, seemed to go along
with it. St Jerome, indeed, said "The whole world

groaned and marvelled to find itself Arian". But the
ordinary people stayed firm. They supported Athanasius
when he was at home, encouraged him when he was in
exile, and with the backing of the monks asserted their
belief in Jesus. Emperors came and went, but Athanasius
died at last in his own diocese surrounded by his loving
people. The struggle against Arianism and Imperial
domination was to be continued by Saints Basil, Gregory
and Ambrose.

SAINT BASIL THE GREAT (330-379)
SAINT GREGORY NAZIANZEN (330-390)

It is difficult to separate these two, while it is important to
distinguish them from each other and from the other
members of their circle. For a start we must be aware that
there were other Basils and Gregories in the story. Basil
"the Great" was born in Cappadocia, in the interior of the
landmass of Asia Minor. His father was also named Basil,
both his grandmother and his sister were called Macrina,
his mother was Emmelia, and his two brothers were Peter,
and Gregory called "of Nyssa". All of these are counted
as saints, and both the younger Macrina and Gregory of
Nyssa have left us important spiritual writings. Then
Basil had a close friend from schooldays called Gregory,
"of Nazianzen", whose father was also Gregory, and also
bishop of Nazianzen. (We must remember that in the
fourth century, if not earlier, it was a common practice for

married men to be ordained on condition that they would henceforth live as celibates; a result was that the priestly vocation tended to run in families.)

The families of Basil and Gregory are collectively known as the "Cappadocian Fathers". During the middle decades of the fourth century they wrote, prayed, studied and debated about the great issues that divided the Church. Gregory of Nazianzen was a poet, leaving long verse explanations of the doctrine that was developing among the friends. Letters passed between them, on personal matters as well as on high points of doctrine, and between the poems and the letters we can see an attractive picture of the domestic friendship of these extraordinary saints.

Basil, after finishing his studies, was called to the monastic life, and founded a community in a remote and charming valley. He wrote to Gregory of Nazianzen describing how pleasant the place was, and urging him to adopt the monastic life himself, but Basil was only granted five years of seclusion before being hurtled into the controversy as Bishop of Caesarea. Despite that, he is acclaimed as the father of Eastern monasticism, and the monastic rules he composed are followed today.

As Bishop of Caesarea, Basil had to contend with the government enforcement of Arianism. He stood up boldly before the local officials, astonishing them with his courage in defending the faith of the Council of Nicaea.

His entire episcopate was disturbed by these controversies, but he still found time, as bishop, to introduce quite remarkable social reforms among his people. He founded schools, hospitals, almshouses, and hostels for travellers, and staffed them with teachers, doctors and nurses, providing social welfare on a scale never seen before. Although a master of contemplative prayer, he was extremely practical in his administration, and so much loved by his people that they lined the streets, weeping, at his funeral.

His teaching was largely worked out in correspondence with his family and friends, particularly Gregory of Nazianzen. This Gregory was far less practical than Basil, and although he reluctantly accepted consecration as bishop, first of Nazianzen and then of Constantinople itself, he was never happy in the role, and joyfully retired back to seclusion in a monastery near his birthplace.

What Basil and Gregory had to contend with was not only the continuing Arian controversy, over whether Jesus truly is God, but the rather neglected topic of the nature and role of the Holy Spirit. The first Council of Nicaea, after defining its teaching on Christ, ended its creed rather lamely, just "and in the Holy Spirit". In some of Basil and Gregory's letters we see how they came to realise that the Holy Spirit is truly God just as much as the Son, but were unsure how the general public would take to this. They could be quite sure the Emperor would not like it. However, as we know, their patient prayer and study enabled them to clarify the doctrine, and develop our familiar faith in the Holy Trinity, One God in Three Persons.

It was the Council of Constantinople in 381, just after Basil's death, that filled in what was lacking at the council of Nicaea. Not only did the Council re-affirm its belief that Jesus is "God from God, light from light, true God from true God, consubstantial with the Father", but it went on to say that the Holy Spirit is "the Lord, the giver of life, who proceeds from the Father, who with the Father and the Son is adored and glorified, who has spoken through the prophets."

For good measure, the Council went on to affirm its faith in "one, holy, catholic and apostolic Church." It was to be centuries before the implications of that line were drawn out, but the affirmation was clear, that there is only One True Church, and the various Arian bodies were not it. We shall see more of this issue in the story of St Ambrose.

It is a little curious that it is Basil and Gregory of Nazianzen who are named as Doctors of the Church, while Gregory of Nyssa was no less part of the circle and no less influential in developing Christian doctrine. But it is the friendship between Basil and the first Gregory that is so attractive, showing us how these great and learned teachers of theology and prayer were also human, fond of reminiscences of schooldays, appreciative of nature and the countryside, of poetry and music. True sanctity does not make us less human, but rather enhances our common humanity. Basil's social action shows how a deep love of God is inseparable from practical love of neighbour.

SAINT JOHN CHRYSOSTOM (345-407)

 In the next generation you might think the Church could settle down, but tensions still existed between Church and State (they have never ceased), and there were still important matters of doctrine to resolve. However, John Chrysostom was a pastoral preacher, not a controversial writer, although his moral teaching soon got him into trouble with the rich and powerful.

John was born in Antioch, one of the great cities of the ancient world, now a desolate ruin in the angle where modern Turkey and Syria meet. After a short training as a monk, he was ordained priest, and rapidly acquired a reputation as a gifted preacher. As a result he was elected bishop of Constantinople in 398, where his preaching came to the notice of the people, but also of the Imperial family.

He was surnamed *Chryso-stom*, "gold-mouth", because of his fluency and facility in public speaking. A great many of his sermons survive, taken down by shorthand writers and edited by him for publication. His technique, used also by many other "Fathers of the Church", was to comment on a book of scripture, verse by verse, in a long series of sermons, typically during the days of Lent. He was not interested in the literal meaning of Scripture, particularly the Old Testament, and tells us nothing about the history and archaeology of Palestine – his interest was in what the Holy Spirit is saying to us now through the Scriptures. St Paul recommends that we should always look for the spiritual meaning rather than the letter of the text, and this spiritual mode of commentary became the characteristic of Catholic orthodoxy. The Scriptures tell us about ourselves, about our relationship to God, and how God moves in our world. In the process, therefore, Chrysostom's sermons tell us a great deal about Catholic doctrine, about the nature of Our Lord, and about prayer. They also seem to be a much more fruitful way of commenting on Holy Scripture than merely talking about the literal meaning of the text, particularly in the Old Testament.

There is also a moral meaning to be drawn out of Scripture. At the end of each sermon, Chrysostom comments on the prevailing behaviour of the people he is addressing, in Antioch or Constantinople, and points to ways in which they might improve. It is clear that the city population is still half pagan, and their behaviour often entirely so. Materialism, worldly status, greed, are the prevailing moods; he castigates their frivolous attachment to sport and amusement, their neglect of the practice of their religion. We learn a lot about the way of life in Imperial Constantinople. Most of all John Chrysostom attacks the idle rich, those who squander vast sums on their own comfort and ostentation, while neglecting the poor, the homeless, the sick, the stranger.

Chrysostom's sermons can make uncomfortable reading today. In his own time they so infuriated the Empress Eudoxia that she was determined to silence him. With the help of some subservient and worldly clergy, she had frivolous and implausible charges trumped up against him, and persuaded her husband the Emperor to have him deposed from his bishopric and banished to the fringes of the Empire. He died from his ill-treatment while being moved from one place of exile to another, a martyr to the integrity of his teaching, though he was never classed as a martyr, possibly for the sake of not antagonising the Imperial family even more. It was to be a persistent problem in the Eastern Church that the Emperors considered themselves above the Church, and would not tolerate any criticism of their autocratic behaviour. Chrysostom's social teaching is still relevant today, and still likely to be unpopular among the powerful and the wealthy.

The four Latin Doctors

St Ambrose, St Jerome, St Augustine, St Gregory the Great

SAINT AMBROSE (340-397)

 Another saint who had trouble with an Empress was Ambrose, Bishop of Milan. He was born at Trier, and trained in the law. He rose to be governor of the province administered from Milan, and was chosen by popular demand to become bishop in 374, even though he was only a catechumen and had not yet been baptised. Milan was now the most important city in the West, since the Imperial administration had abandoned the unhealthy city of Rome. The Empire was divided for most of the fourth century, and the power in the West was in the hands of the Empress, Justina, who supported the Arian heresy, largely because her power-base was in the Gothic mercenaries she employed.

Ambrose came into direct conflict with Justina when she demanded that a Catholic church in Milan should be handed over for Arian worship. Ambrose refused, and in a surprisingly modern demonstration of protest, occupied the church with his supporters, who sang psalms according to the "Ambrosian" tones until the soldiers of the Empress could bear it no more, and she was forced to give in.

When it came to doctrine, Ambrose had to complete in the West what Athanasius and the Cappadocians were doing in the East. Simultaneously with the great Council of Constantinople, Ambrose directed a Western council at Aquileia, which affirmed the faith of Nicaea, and established the orthodox and Catholic faith as the religion of the Empire.

After discreet assassinations and removal of unwanted Emperors, the Empire finally came back together under the powerful Theodosius. He also had to be tamed by Ambrose, who ruled firmly that "the emperor is within the Church, he is not above it – we may not bear the sword, you may not carry incense." Each has authority in his own sphere, it is the duty of the bishop to tell the Emperor what is right and wrong, the duty of the Emperor to rule according to justice and enforce the right. This teaching of Ambrose remained firm in the West, despite repeated attempts by kings and Emperors to overthrow it: the Church is free, and Church teaching is the responsibility of the bishops as successors of the Apostles. The State is responsible for supporting and protecting the Church, but no worldly power has the right to make decisions on matters of faith or morals. Here is the contrast with the East, where by and large the

Emperors dominated the Church, and continually tried to meddle in matters of doctrine.

As well as leaving teaching of lasting value on the relationship between Church and State, Ambrose left writings on spiritual matters, doctrinal and catechetical texts. He is best remembered, however, as the author of a number of hymns, in highly accomplished Latin. These and others inspired by his example, formed part of the Divine Office of the Church for the next sixteen hundred years, and versions of them are still in use.

SAINT JEROME (345-420)

 It is always encouraging to find a saint with obvious faults and flaws of character. If St Jerome can become a saint, there is hope for all of us. He was obviously a very difficult person to live with, and his correspondence shows a waspish anger which soured his relationships with many of his former friends. Sanctity comes through combating faults, and persevering in trying to love God and neighbour; there is no sanctity in never having anything to combat!

He came from what is now Croatia, but studied in Rome, until he fled to the desert of Syria to try to get away from temptation. This was not successful – the memory of girls he had known in Rome pursued him wherever he went, and the other hermits disliked him and objected to his presence in their desert. (The story of his encounter with a lion is, alas, a mistake; it really belongs to St Gerasimus). With more sense he returned to Rome, and worked as secretary to Pope St Damasus between 382 and 383.

It was Damasus who encouraged him to work on the Scriptures, recognising his skill with languages. After the Pope's death, Jerome retired to Bethlehem, surrounded by research-assistants such as St Paula and her daughter St Eustochium, and devoted the rest of his life to study.

With access to manuscripts in Hebrew, Aramaic and Greek that have long ago crumbled into powder, Jerome was in a good position to establish a "critical text" of the Bible, choosing carefully which version to follow when manuscripts disagreed. He produced a Latin version of most of the Bible, known as the "Vulgate", which remains the basis of the authoritative version of the Bible for the Western Church. He also wrote commentaries on many of the most important books of the Bible, going through the text, giving learned notes on the original languages, explaining knotty problems of translation, and bringing out the spiritual meaning.

He wrote letters to many people, in East and West, and these well-preserved letters give us a valuable picture of life in the early fifth century, as well as dealing with matters of monastic life, spirituality, prayer – and the faults of his correspondents. But his lasting importance is in the emphasis he gave to Holy Scripture, for in his famous phrase, "ignorance of the Scriptures is ignorance of Christ".

SAINT AUGUSTINE (354-430)

 A giant figure, much admired, and much reviled, Augustine has influenced the Western Church through his writings more than anyone else. Although his mother was a Christian, his father refused to let him be baptised, saying he should "make up his own mind". He drifted into a cult, and only in adult life found himself drawn more and more to his mother's faith. The story of his wild youth, his involvement with the Manichaean cult, and his conversion, is told in the *Confessions*, the first great Christian autobiography. His mother St Monica died happy, knowing that her wayward son had found his way home at last.

Returning to his native Africa, Augustine adopted a monastic way of life for a few years, before being elected bishop of Hippo on the north coast in 396. Here he taught, preached and catechised, wrote innumerable letters and commentaries on Scripture, and combated the various strange heresies that sprung up at the time. Some put about the idea that there should be a separate "African" church: Augustine insisted that the Church must be one, worldwide, uniting people of all nations. Some thought that it was possible to earn our own salvation by good works: Augustine emphasised that without the grace of God we can do nothing. Some thought that the disasters which overwhelmed the Roman Empire in his time, including the sack of Rome itself, were to be blamed on the Christians: Augustine explained that God offers us prosperity and peace in the next world, not in this.

Augustine's teaching was misused much later, and terrible mistakes were made in the sixteenth century by those who read too much of him, but taken in the context of the time, his complex doctrine about nature and grace, and about the Holy Trinity, proved to be the basis of all subsequent Catholic teaching. From his letters has been extracted a rule of life for canons and friars, who have helped to perpetuate his memory and preserve his vast output of writings. He died in old age, while his city was being besieged by an army of Germanic warriors (Vandals), and the flourishing church in his native land was wiped out, but his books were rescued and brought to Europe to dominate Catholic thought for over a thousand years.

SAINT GREGORY THE GREAT (540-604)

 A good bit later than the other great Doctors comes St Gregory, Pope from 590 to his death in 604. It was a time when Roman power in the West had failed, and the Emperors in the East had less and less authority in the West. Into the vacuum came Gregory, trained as a lawyer, professed as a monk, sent as a Papal envoy in Constantinople, skilled in administration and diplomacy, and elected Pope when he only really wanted to be a monk again. He found himself obliged to organise civil government in Rome and its neighbourhood, since no one else could do it, and so laid the basis of the independence of the Popes from political control. Because of this independence, the Roman Church was free to grow and to develop its teaching, in a way that was never possible in the East, even though there were many times when the Popes had to fight hard to retain that freedom.

St Gregory's administration of the Church resulted in an immense number of letters written to men and women of all sorts in all countries. Some are about internal Church matters, some on matters of state. They give a fascinating picture of the life of the period, as well as containing practical, doctrinal, and spiritual advice. He is well remembered for sending the younger Saint Augustine to evangelise south-east England, backing him up with notes of introduction to contacts on the way, and letters of encouragement and advice on the mission. Like most of the Fathers, Gregory also wrote commentaries on Scripture, which emerged from courses of sermons: the most influential was the immense commentary on the Book of Job which is a treatise on moral theology. Influential also was his little book of advice to those in authority in the Church, the *Pastoral Care*, required reading for bishops to this day. In many ways Gregory reformed the office and work of the Popes so that it was fit to serve the Church during the rapidly changing political circumstances of the next few centuries; but he claimed for himself and his successors the title only of "servant of the servants of God."

The fathers of the first millennium

After the original four Latin and four Greek Doctors, we must turn to those who have only been recognised as Doctors in modern times. Most of them can be looked at more briefly. We begin with a number of others from the First Millennium, always classed as "Fathers of the Church", though they were only recognised as "Doctors" much later – Saints Ephraem the Syrian, Hilary of Poitiers, Cyril of Jerusalem, Cyril of Alexandria, Leo the Great, Peter Chrysologus, Isidore of Seville, Bede of Jarrow, and John Damascene.

SAINT EPHRAEM THE SYRIAN (306-73)

A permanent deacon, St Ephraem spent much of his life in the city of Edessa where a famous theological school trained clergy to serve the Syriac-speaking population of the Middle East. This was at the time of the Arian controversies, when it was vital to give clear orthodox teaching about the nature of Our Lord. Ephraem's original contribution was to write metrical hymns which incorporated important doctrine, so that people would remember the teaching while they sang the hymns. Even in his prose writings he used flowery and poetic language, to make his message attractive. Poetry is always difficult to translate, but his works circulated in Greek, Armenian and Latin versions, and a few of his hymns such as "Virgin, wholly marvellous" have even found their way into English hymnbooks. He was proclaimed Doctor of the Church in 1920.

SAINT HILARY OF POITIERS (315-68)

Another fourth-century champion of orthodoxy, Saint Hilary met Athanasius during one of his periodic times in exile, and was able to confirm that what was being taught in the West was absolutely in accord with Athanasius' teaching and that of the Council of Nicaea. Hilary himself, Bishop of Poitiers in Roman Gaul since 350, was sent into exile in the East, where he was doing so much to strengthen the Catholic cause that the Arians themselves sent him back home. While in the East he had picked up the idea of writing hymns to expound Catholic doctrine, which he taught to his people. He also wrote on doctrine, notably on the Holy Trinity, and built up the organisation of his diocese in an age of rapid evangelisation. He was granted the title of Doctor in 1851.

SAINT CYRIL OF JERUSALEM (315-87)

Cyril also had to contend with the Arian crisis, and was three times sent into exile. As bishop of Jerusalem from 349 to his death, he ruled over a small but extremely prestigious congregation, which needed much pastoral care. For their benefit he composed his Catechetical Instructions, to explain the three sacraments of initiation, Baptism, Confirmation and the Eucharist, and to bring out their true meaning. These Instructions are invaluable for they show clearly how the faith of the fourth century in the birthplace of the Church is the same that the Church has proclaimed ever since. For this reason he was acclaimed as a Doctor in 1883.

SAINT CYRIL OF ALEXANDRIA (376-444)

Like St Jerome, Cyril of Alexandria was a saint with a temper – if he can be a saint, anyone can. His temper and his violent and vigorous action were deployed in a worthy cause: the final triumph of clear and correct teaching about the nature of Our Lord and the Holy Trinity. Even after the Arian crisis seemed to have been overcome, there were mistaken preachers who failed to understand the message that "the Word was made flesh" – they thought Our Lord was not really human, or that the human being Jesus was not the same person as the eternal

Christ, or that their natures were so blurred together that he was neither God nor man. Cyril taught that He was, and is, true God and true Man, and because of that Our Lady can truly be called the Mother of God. This teaching was accepted at the Council of Ephesus in 431. It is reassuring to see that in old age he became gentler and more conciliatory, and was eventually recognised as a Doctor of the Church in 1882.

SAINT LEO THE GREAT (390-461)

Very few men (and even fewer women) have been honoured with the title "the Great", but Pope Leo is among them. In the middle of the fifth century the Western Empire was falling apart, civil government breaking down, and new more vigorous nations were moving in. Among them were the Huns, led by their doughty chieftain Attila. It fell to Pope Leo to meet Attila at the gates of Rome, and to succeed where armies had failed, in negotiating a peaceful withdrawal, and sparing the city from the attentions of a conquering army. Shortly afterwards he had to repeat these delicate negotiations with the Vandals, who did enter the city, but refrained from sacking it. It was this skilful diplomacy that earned him the affection of the Roman people, and enabled him to consolidate the role of the Papacy in guiding the world on the ways of peace.

But at the same time the faith was under threat yet again from distorted teaching – the achievement of St Cyril of Alexandria in defining the faith at Ephesus was being over-exaggerated by those who thought the two natures of God and Man had been fused into one in the person of Christ. This may seem like too refined a point to be significant, but the effect of this error (the "Monophysite" heresy) was to undermine the reality of Our Lord's humanity again. If he is not truly human, we cannot truly relate to him, and he does not truly share our nature. Too busy saving Rome to attend the Council of Chalcedon (451) in person, Pope Leo dashed off a letter stating the Catholic doctrine clearly and succinctly. When it was read out at the Council the bishops sprang to their feet and shouted "this is the voice of Peter!" The resulting Definition of Chalcedon incorporated Leo's letter (known as his "Tome") in a beautifully poetic statement about Our Lord, true God and true Man, consubstantial with the Father according to his divinity, and consubstantial with us according to his humanity. He is thus truly the link between earth and heaven, and because we share his human nature, he opens for us the way to the Father.

Thus Pope Leo did not only serve his people in a practical way by safeguarding the City, he served us in a doctrinal way by guiding the faith of the world. For this reason he was granted the title of Doctor of the Church by Pope Benedict XIV in 1754.

SAINT PETER CHRYSOLOGUS (400-450)

If Leo is an obvious candidate for the title of Doctor, Peter Chrysologus is less so. He was bishop of Ravenna in north eastern Italy from about 435, and noted as an eloquent preacher. His soubriquet *Chryso-logus* means "golden words", though the surviving sermons are not particularly distinguished. Maybe, like Newman, it all depended on hearing him in person. His themes are simple Gospel teaching, his only involvement in the controversies of his time a strong affirmation of the supremacy of the teaching of Pope Leo the Great against the Monophysites. Yet he was awarded the title of Doctor before Leo, in 1729.

SAINT ISIDORE OF SEVILLE (560-636)

 The Arian heresy, which we thought we had seen off at the Council of Constantinople in 381, continued to thrive among the younger nations of Europe, who had simplified it into an acceptance of Jesus as merely a good man, a teacher and example. It was left to St Isidore and his brother St Leander to polish off the last of the Arians by negotiating a reconciliation with the Visigoths and Vandals in Spain and North Africa. This was probably the last time that a major heretical denomination was successfully reconciled to the Catholic Church. The two brothers were bishops of

Seville one after another for half a century, which gave them the opportunity to consolidate the Faith in Spain and to organise religious life there.

Isidore is best remembered for his encyclopaedia, the *Etymologies*, a glossary of all sorts of terminology, both religious and secular, and other works of systematic scholarship, useful for instructing a newly converted nation. He was awarded his Doctorate in 1722.

SAINT BEDE OF JARROW (673-735)

 The only English Doctor of the Church (so far), Bede is remembered above all as a historian. In fact he wrote a great deal more than his famous *Ecclesiastical History of the English Nation*, producing deeply spiritual commentaries on some of the more unpromising parts of the Old Testament, such as the instructions to Moses on building the Tabernacle. He also produced an amazingly complicated work of mathematics and astronomy, intended practically to enable anyone to calculate the date of Easter.

But it is as historian that we honour him. He passed almost his entire life in the twin monasteries of Wearmouth and Jarrow, observing the monastic rule, and corresponding with many scholars throughout Europe to collect the materials for his writing. He was the first to recognise the importance of Church History, and incidentally one of the first to use the now-familiar system of reckoning the years since the Birth of Our Lord. Many attacks on the Church, then and now, are based on stories from the past, misunderstood, distorted, and manipulated to discredit the Church of the present. Bede showed how an accurate and well-researched account of the past can help us to brush away the cobwebs of false history, and serve the Church for the future. He was greatly revered throughout Europe even in his own time, called "venerable" while still alive, but not recognised as a Doctor of the Church until 1899.

SAINT JOHN DAMASCENE (676-749)

Contemporary with Bede but at the opposite end of the Christian world was John, born at Damascus in Syria, when it was already under Muslim rule. After a time serving the Caliph Abdul Malek at court, John retired to a monastery in the wilderness between Jerusalem and the Dead Sea. Here he was able to write – and the great paradox of his life is that he was free in a Muslim state to write theology that would not have been permitted in Christian Constantinople. For the eastern Empire was in the grip of a strange whim of the Emperors, the "Iconoclastic" heresy. Possibly influenced by Islam, the Emperor Leo III decided to prohibit any form of representational art, and enforced this law with astonishing brutality. John of Damascus explained that since our faith is based on the fundamental fact that the Word became flesh, material objects can now be made holy, and that since the whole of human nature is caught up into the divinity it is appropriate to represent that humanity in art. The eventual triumph of his teaching is celebrated in the East as the "Feast of Orthodoxy", though it was not finally attained until 842. John also taught a great deal about the honour due to Our Lady, so that he guided our understanding of two common characteristics of Orthodox and Catholic Christianity, the respect due to icons and sacred images, and the honour of Our Lady. He also wrote hymns, such as "Come, ye faithful, raise the strain", and "The Day of Resurrection." His Doctorate was awarded in 1890.

The scholars of the middle ages

The dawn of the Second Millennium saw the tragic separation of East and West, still unresolved despite persistent efforts on the part of many Popes. Now the Development of Christian Doctrine is apparent to us mostly from Western sources; such theological developments as the East has produced are little known in the Western Church. In what we call the Middle Ages we meet another group of Doctors – Saints Peter Damian, Anselm, Bernard of Clairvaux, Anthony of Padua, Albert the Great, Bonaventure, Thomas Aquinas, and Catherine of Siena.

SAINT PETER DAMIAN (1007-1072)

The tenth century was a terrible time, when the rich and powerful had gained control over the Church, and forced their unwanted children on the people as priests, bishops and even Popes. The dawn of a new millennium was an occasion for reform, and during the eleventh century the Church shook herself free of the rich, and reformed the lives of the clergy. These reforms are remembered under the name of Pope Gregory VII (1073-85) but the inspiration behind them came largely from his friend Peter Damian.

Peter spent much of his life as a monk in the strict reformed order of Camaldoli, where he developed a rigorous asceticism that was the only answer to the decadence and worldliness of the time. Later as Cardinal Bishop of Ostia he had a chance to put his projected reforms into practice. He saw that when the clergy are decadent and corrupt there is little hope for the laity, and wrote very vigorously against the two prevailing vices.

One was a widespread disregard for purity, both within and outside of marriage, known as "Nicolaitism" after Nicolas, the apostate deacon from the New Testament (Acts 6:5, Apoc. 2:15). The discipline of the Church for centuries had been that the higher clergy should either be unmarried, or, if married, should separate from their wives when they were ordained subdeacon. This separation was not always being observed, even by bishops and Popes. Part of the reform was a gradual move towards ordaining only unmarried men or widowers except in exceptional circumstances. (This tied in well with the developing theology of Matrimony, which now came to be seen as a Sacrament, a good thing in its own right, not to be broken up for ordination.) Peter Damian wrote a stream of hard-hitting pamphlets designed to recall the clergy to their obligations.

The other vice was "Simony", named after Simon Magus (Acts 8:18-24) who tried to buy the right to ordination. The office of bishop in particular had become a matter of commerce, much in demand since a bishop had access to considerable funds, and it was bought and sold among the powerful families of Europe. Again Peter's pamphlets denounced the evil vigorously. The great reforms which Popes and Councils managed to achieve in both these areas owed much to the ideas and teaching of Peter Damian, which is why he was declared a Doctor of the Church in 1828, and in the process automatically canonized.

SAINT ANSELM OF CANTERBURY (1033-1109)

 Born in Lombardy, trained as a monk in Normandy, and appointed Archbishop of Canterbury, Anselm reminds us of just how international the Church was in the days of the great reforms. In England he was kept busy opposing the Norman kings who wanted control over the Church; in the struggle for the freedom of the Church, Anselm had to go into exile more than once. Despite this he was able to promote reforms in the lives of the clergy, and also campaigned vigorously against slavery.

However he is remembered more for his writings than his pastoral work. He is usually considered the first of the

"Scholastics" or "Schoolmen", theologians who approached doctrine in a systematic manner. The older style, that of the Fathers, had been to incorporate their theological thought in commentaries on the Scriptures; Anselm began with a reasoned argument about theology set out in a logical order, and used Scripture and the Fathers to support his argument. This became the standard procedure thenceforth.

In particular, Anselm examined the two great questions, how do we know God exists, and why did God become Man. Neither of his answers are entirely satisfactory: the "ontological" argument for the existence of God is that He must exist because there must be something greater than anything we can imagine. St Thomas Aquinas showed that this will not do (though it almost convinced Bertrand Russell). On the reason for the Incarnation, Anselm introduced the now familiar theory of atonement; that Christ came to pay the debt to God that we owe for our sins. Again St Thomas had to correct the misleading impression that somehow the Father and the Son are opposed to each other, whereas in reality it is the love of the entire Holy Trinity that directs our salvation. Despite these loose ends, Anselm's theology was sufficiently important for him to be declared a Doctor of the Church, and in the process a Saint, in 1720.

SAINT BERNARD OF CLAIRVAUX (1090-1153)

 If Anselm was the first of the Schoolmen, his younger contemporary Bernard was the last of the Fathers, for he continued to expound his teaching in the course of sermons on the Scriptures. Born in Burgundy, he was one of the first monks to join the newly reformed Abbey of Cîteaux, and by his effective leadership rapidly became the greatest promoter of a monastic reform which would sweep across Europe. They followed the Rule of St Benedict to the letter, earning their keep by hard work, devoting their time to prayer and meditation. Like many who sought peace and obscurity in a monastery, Bernard soon became the advisor and counsellor of kings and popes, unafraid to write letters of stern advice and rebuke to the Pope when needed. In public affairs he tried to prevent the unjust treatment of the Jews, and to organise help for Christians under oppression by Islamic rulers. (In both of these he was unsuccessful.)

His writings are what endure. His sermons and meditations speak persuasively of the love of God, and of how through prayer we can be united to that love, a love that shows itself in our affection for each other. In four volumes of commentary on the Song of Songs he only gets half way through the book, but tells us an enormous amount about the spiritual life. In his sermons for Advent we find some of the most beautiful reflections on Our Lady. One of his hymns is familiar as "Daily, daily, sing to Mary." St Bernard also made it easier to understand St Joseph's holiness by pointing out that his reaction to Mary's expectation was not angry jealousy but humble reverence and awe. He was unashamed in speaking about his affection for his monks, and his letters are full of human touches, surprising in one so rigorous in his own life. The gentle and even humorous style in which he wrote makes him easy to read and profitable today, for laypeople as much as for monks. He was awarded his Doctorate in 1830.

SAINT ANTHONY OF PADUA (1195-1231)

Although he has become one of the most popular saints in recent times, it is not often realised that St Anthony has left us important writings, mostly in the form of sermons. He was actually Portuguese, born in Lisbon, and only joined the Franciscans after years as a canon regular in Coimbra. As a friar, he preached at great risk in Morocco, and with greater effect in Europe. As ever, the need was for hard-hitting sermons on personal reform, turning away from sin, correcting the vices of the clergy and issuing stern rebukes to the rich who exploited the poor. He travelled widely through France and Italy, preaching, but his association with Padua is simply because he happened to die there.

There was also at this time difficulty with a weird sect that had set up in the south of France, the Cathars (a recurrence of the old sect of the Manichees), who taught that all matter was evil, and in particular that marriage was evil, and that unless you joined their sect there was no hope of salvation, but only an endless cycle of rebirth. The more extreme ones thought that all food and drink were evil too, and that the best way to get to heaven was to starve yourself and your family to death. They rejected all sacraments (because they involve material things like water, bread and wine), and repudiated all civil government except in the hands of their own cult members. These people were really not very nice, and it is not surprising that civil governments acted against them – but St Anthony met them with sermons full of reasoned argument and Scriptural proofs that God created the world and it was very good, that he so loved the world that he sent his only Son that the world should be saved. St Anthony's sermons were so effective that he was called the "hammer of heretics". (In this he was joined by St Dominic, who founded his Order of Preachers to explain the faith in charity). Despite his enormous popularity, St Anthony was only declared a Doctor of the Church in 1946.

SAINT ALBERT THE GREAT (1206-1280)

Although St Dominic himself never got his Doctorate, some of his great followers did, beginning with St Albert. Born in southern Germany, Albert studied in Padua, and there joined the new and fast-growing Order of Preachers. After further studies in Paris, he settled in Cologne and directed the studies for the entire Dominican order. He is of enormous importance in that he was probably the last person who was able to study all the sciences in depth, as well as theology and philosophy – as knowledge grows it becomes impossible for any one person to be fully up to date in even one science, let alone the whole range of physics, astronomy, chemistry, biology, physiology, geography, geology and botany. St Albert lectured and wrote on all of these, and was able to integrate them into his theology.

The key to reconciling faith and science is in the philosophy: Albert discovered the works of Aristotle and realised that his approach solved many of the problems which had been causing division over the previous few centuries. In particular, Aristotle showed how matter and spirit fit together in God's creation, so that the soul is not something from outside, merely inserted into the body, but is the form of the body itself. Hence matter is good, the body is holy, marriage is holy, and the study of material creation is all part of the study of God in his works. All these ideas were taken up and developed by his great pupil Thomas Aquinas. It is perhaps surprising that Albert was only given his Doctorate, and in the process declared a saint, in 1931.

SAINT BONAVENTURE (1217-1274)

 The Franciscans and the Dominicans have always engaged in mostly friendly competition in preaching and bringing people to the love of God. Bonaventure was a Franciscan, an Italian who studied in Paris and preached throughout Italy and France like St Anthony. Although St Francis himself tried to live a life of extreme simplicity, it did not take long before his followers became learned and scholarly, knowing that people demand reasons for the hope that is in us, and that the good preacher must be able to convince the mind as well as the heart. Bonaventure was close enough to the ideals of St Francis that he lived in simplicity, and was found washing the dishes when they came to make him a cardinal. He wrote the *Journey of the Soul to God*, on the spiritual life, explaining how mystical theology in prayer unites us to the Father, as well as many other works on prayer and spirituality. At the end of his life he took part in the Council of Lyons (St Albert was there too) which achieved re-union between Greeks and Latins, though tragically only for a short time.

He was declared a Doctor of the Church by Pope Sixtus V (himself a Franciscan) in 1588.

SAINT THOMAS AQUINAS (1225-1274)

 The greatest of all the Scholastic theologians, Thomas of Aquino, built on the work of his teacher St Albert to bring together all knowledge of God and how he relates to us, and explained this in an astonishing number of lengthy publications. He taught in several different places in Italy and France, and died on his way to that disappointing Council of Lyons. His massive work the *Summa Theologica* is an (unfinished) encyclopaedia of religious knowledge, asking every question, exploring every point of view, considering every opinion. The part left unfinished can be made up by reference to other works, in which he looks at all sorts of disputed questions, as well as commenting on the epistles of St Paul. All subsequent theology has been in debt to him, and many errors can be corrected by referring back to him, even in our own time. In particular he taught us about the Blessed Sacrament, and showed how the creative power of God is at work in the *transubstantiation* of bread and wine into the Body and Blood of Christ. Of course there has been development of doctrine since, but St Thomas's teaching enables us to see how that development has grown organically out of what was said before.

The key to the theology and philosophy of Thomas Aquinas was his life of prayer – to contemplate, and to pass on to others what contemplation has revealed. Because of that he was invited to compose the Mass and Office for the new feast of Corpus Christi – the texts he chose, and the poems he wrote to go with them are of outstanding beauty, such as the familiar *Tantum ergo*. The hymn *Adoro te devote*, "Godhead here in hiding", is also his. He was the first to be declared a Doctor of the Church by a Pope, in 1567 when Pius V (a Dominican himself) extended to him the title which only the original four Latins and four Greeks had held before that.

SAINT CATHERINE OF SIENA (1347-1379)

 Another Dominican, Saint Catherine is the only one of these Doctors to achieve the additional rank of Patron of Europe. Yet the main reason for this is that she was so energetic in correcting and reproving the Popes. It was a time when the Church was divided, with rival Popes based in Rome and Avignon: it has never been quite certainly established which was the true Pope, and saints were found on both sides. Catherine's energies were thrown on the side of Pope Urban VI (in Rome), and she implored him again and again to resolve the crisis. He paid little attention, and the division was not overcome until the Council of Constance in the next century, but St

Catherine's efforts towards reform of the Church were long remembered. She also worked hard to make peace between the squabbling little states of Italy.

Her theological importance, however, lies in the realm of mystical theology: she had many spiritual experiences which taught her much about the union of the human soul with Christ. She expressed this under the image of a "mystical marriage", a theme which was taken up and developed by later spiritual writers. She had a wide correspondence, and was supported by a loyal group of followers, the "Caterinati". Enormously popular in her lifetime and afterwards, she had to wait until 1970 for her Doctorate.

The early modern reformers

The Middle Ages are often called the "Ages of Faith", because despite the occasional division in the Church, and the endless struggle against vice and worldliness, it was a time when almost everyone in Western Europe considered themselves to be Catholic Christians. This unity was violently disrupted in the sixteenth century, beginning a long series of Wars of Religion, at the end of which much of the North was lost to the Church, and the Muslims took advantage of the confusion to advance well into Central Europe, but the Catholic Church grew and spread far through the Southern Hemisphere. A number of great saints were involved in upholding the great reforms which the Church underwent, while the kings of the earth, the rich and powerful, were tearing whole sections of Christendom away to subject them to their own domination. The Doctors of this Catholic Reform period are Saints Teresa of Ávila, John of the Cross, Peter Canisius, Robert Bellarmine, Lawrence of Brindisi, and Francis de Sales.

SAINT TERESA OF ÁVILA (1515-82)

 Short, but traditionally built, St Teresa of Jesus was one of the greatest teachers of prayer in the history of the Church. She became a Carmelite nun in a convent just outside the walls of her home town of Ávila, and lived there in reasonable comfort, despite ill health, until her forties, when she experienced such an awareness of God's love that she felt called to a more austere life. Despite considerable opposition from other nuns, she founded a new convent, St Joseph's, where the sisters could live the Carmelite life to the full, in simplicity and seclusion. The reform spread, and she herself had to travel up and down Spain making new foundations, struggling for the recognition of the convents as part of a Reformed branch of the Carmelite Order. This branch came to be known as the "Discalced" ("without shoes"), and eventually won its independence from the "Mitigated" branch of the Order. In all this she was assisted by St John of the Cross.

While engaged in these energetic works, Teresa managed to find time to write her own story in the *Life* and the *Foundations*, as well as an elementary treatise on prayer, the *Way of Perfection*, and a deeper exploration of mystical prayer, the *Interior Castle*. She also wrote a great many letters, in which practical and humorous comments are interspersed with reflections of the most sublime spirituality. For the new foundations she concerned herself about roofing, drains and food supplies (she loved her food), as well as how to deal with difficult nuns and more difficult benefactors. Her family also caused her anxiety, and it is obvious that the effect of the love of God in her life was to make her more concerned for the welfare of others. She writes without pretensions about the extraordinary things that happened to her at the beginning of her spiritual awakening, particularly the experience known as the "Transverberation", when she felt as if her heart was pierced by a burning arrow of love. (This feeling of burning in the heart, the *incendium amoris*, is common to many saints, expressed in various ways.) Yet she paid little attention to the extraordinary, choosing to lead people on the ordinary path towards perfection that consists in being open to God's love, and allowing the love of God to flow through towards other people. Her writings were translated into English soon after she died, and have remained popular ever since. At a time of religious warfare, Teresa brought reform to religious life and a teaching on prayer that drew people back to God. She was granted her Doctorate in 1970.

SAINT JOHN OF THE CROSS (1542-91)

Saint Teresa hoped to find a Carmelite Friar to help her in the way of reform – in the end she had to settle for "half a friar" as she called St John of the Cross, who was even shorter than she was. He was very active in the practical reform of the Order, and the struggle to established a Discalced branch for men as well as women. In this he suffered considerable persecution from the Mitigated friars, and was imprisoned in Toledo for nine months. However he took advantage of this enforced retreat to begin his great and poetic mystical writings, which went through several versions before they eventually appeared as the *Ascent of Mount Carmel*, the *Dark Night of the Soul*, the *Spiritual Canticle*, and the *Living Flame*. Drawing on the imagery of the Song of Songs, like many mystic writers before him, St John shows us how it is only when we are prepared to demand nothing for ourselves that God can give us everything.

He explores the very common problem that people find it difficult to pray, and may even feel cut off from God in their prayer life, plagued by distractions and depressed by anxiety. In this "dark night" it is John of the Cross who teaches us to recognise the "shade of His hand", and to gain the strength to persevere in prayer even when we feel God has abandoned us. It is in our own nothingness that his power is greatest, as Our Lady and St Paul had exclaimed before. St John's writings are perhaps less accessible than those of St Teresa, but they are of enormous value in helping people through the difficulties of a life of prayer. It is for this reason that he was made a Doctor of the Church in 1926.

SAINT PETER CANISIUS (1521-97)

If Teresa and John laid the foundations of modern spirituality, it was Peter Canisius who did most to correct the odd ideas that were circulating in Europe by giving sound practical catechesis. A Dutch theologian who joined the new Society of Jesus, he dedicated his life to preaching and teaching all over southern Germany, Austria and Bohemia. He took part in the great reforming Council of Trent, and organised schools and colleges to restore education in areas where the wars of religion had destroyed so much. He worked in particular in Prague, Augsburg, Innsbruck and Fribourg (where he died), and to him is attributed the restoration of Catholic Christianity in those areas, for he could win people over by his courteous and reasoned explanations of the Faith. He travelled enormous distances on foot to preach missions in parishes and remote areas. Among his copious writings it is the Catechism that stands out, for in this he made the faith accessible to everyone, whatever age or background. He was acclaimed Doctor of the Church and thereby canonised in 1925.

SAINT ROBERT BELLARMINE (1542-1621)

While Peter Canisius was tramping the lanes of Bohemia, another Jesuit, St Robert Bellarmine, remained at the centre of affairs in Rome. He taught in the Jesuit college in Rome, and was a key member of the Curia for many years. His research and writing was on the controversial issues of the time, and he corresponded with many dissident Christians in the hope of explaining Catholic doctrine to them. In particular he looked at the whole issue of authority in the Church, and at the nature of the Church itself. He showed how the Church must be One, as we proclaim in the Creed, and that a Christ-given teaching authority is necessary. But he also wrote on spiritual matters, commenting on the Psalms in relation to the life of prayer. He was canonised and declared Doctor in 1930.

SAINT LAWRENCE OF BRINDISI (1559-1622)

Perhaps the most unexpected of the Doctors is Lawrence of Brindisi, a Capuchin friar who preached in many parts of Europe, and left learned comments on the Scriptures. He is perhaps the least known of the Doctors of the Church; most of his writings were not published until the twentieth century. They show a profound understanding of the role and significance of the Virgin Mary as a model for the Church and the Christian life. During the struggle to liberate central Europe from Turkish occupation, he accompanied the armies in the field, acting as a military chaplain under fire. He was declared Doctor of the Church in 1959.

SAINT FRANCIS DE SALES (1567-1622)

There is no difficulty in understanding why St Francis de Sales is a Doctor of the Church: his writings are of enormous value and are widely read in many languages. From Savoy, a small country between France and Italy, he was greatly influenced by the Oratory of St Philip Neri, and was trying to form an Oratory in Thonon when he was made Bishop of Geneva. The city was then in the hands of a violently anti-Catholic sect, and he was unable to visit it openly, but he made a base across the lake and preached so effectively that he won back a large proportion of his people to the faith. The idea he had to combat was that God wills to send the majority of people to eternal torment through no fault of their own, and to save only a few people whether they like it or not. This monstrous distortion of the Gospel was not only found outside the Church but had even infected the Catholic Church in France (under the label of Jansenism). The message of St Francis is about the love of God, that God really yearns for all men to be saved, and that the redemption is the loving work of Father, Son and Holy Spirit together.

Hence his most important book, *A Treatise on the Love of God*. He also strongly promoted the lay apostolate, training lay men and women in prayer, and the knowledge of the faith, so that they could spread the message of God's love to their bewildered neighbours. Hence his other really important book, *The Introduction to the Devout Life*. With the help of his close friend St Jeanne Françoise de Chantal, he founded the Visitation Order, through which came the revelation of the Sacred Heart, how much God loves us with a human heart. In a huge number of letters, to people of all sorts, St Francis teaches us much about prayer and how to live a truly spiritual life no matter what our circumstances. He was finally granted his Doctorate in 1877.

Into the age of revolution

A result of the Wars of Religion was that many people in Europe decided to reject religion altogether, looking to "reason" or "science" as the answer to life. The so-called "Age of Enlightenment" (really of gathering darkness) led directly to the worst excesses of the Revolution, which swept through North America, France, Italy, Spain, Portugal, and finally Russia. Saints who tried to bring sanity to an anti-religious world included Saints Alphonsus de' Liguori and Thérèse of Lisieux, our last two Doctors.

SAINT ALPHONSUS DE' LIGUORI (1696-1787)

 Alphonsus began his career as a preacher, particularly in country districts of the Kingdom of Naples, the southern half of Italy. To extend this work he founded a congregation of priests, now well-known as the Redemptorists. They specialised in parish missions, visiting remote areas where ignorance or laxity had left people with very vague ideas about Christianity, and explaining the Gospel in simple terms to bring people back to the Sacraments and the love of God. The

Kingdom of Naples had been infected with the severe moralising of the Jansenists, and to counteract that, St Alphonsus wrote and taught a moral theology of patience and moderation. Those who had been driven to despair by the impossible demands of the rigorists found hope and forgiveness through his teaching. He also wrote much about Our Lady, including the hymn, "O Mother blest". St Alphonsus had to suffer much, especially from members of his own congregation, but it is for his moral theology that he was awarded his doctorate in 1871, the only Doctor of the Church to be proclaimed as such within a hundred years of his death.

SAINT THÉRÈSE OF LISIEUX (1873-97)

 Perhaps the best-known and best loved of all the Doctors of the Church is the "Little Flower", whose teachings appeal to millions who would find the closely-argued theology of the other Doctors too much for them. Born into a middle-class family in Normandy, she had to contend against temptations to silliness and sentimentality in her heroic struggle towards the love of Christ. Like her older sisters she was called to religious life, in the Carmel of Lisieux, where she died young. She might have remained as obscure and unknown in death as she had hoped to be in life, were it not for the autobiographical writings which she wrote, under obedience. They proved to be a quite extraordinary success, even in the heavily edited version first given to the world. The authentic text, released in the 1950s, shows the strength of character she gained by her surrender to the love of God. She taught the "little way" of simple trust in God, doing ordinary things in an extraordinary way. It was in her centenary year, 1997, that she was proclaimed as the latest and youngest of the Doctors.

Will there be more?

There has been much speculation over the possibility of other Doctors of the Church being recognised and proclaimed. The criteria that the Church looks for are five, labelled rather ponderously as these: Charism of Wisdom, Mature Sapiental Synthesis, Authentic Spiritual Mastery and Christian Witness, Ecclesial Sources, and Wide Diffusion and Beneficial Influence. Which being interpreted means that the potential Doctor must have something really significant to say, and express it in a useful manner, he must be a holy person, fully in accord with the teaching of the Church, and have been a good influence to a large range of the faithful. We may wonder whether some of those declared in the past quite fit these criteria, but ultimately responsibility rests on the Pope.

What we have noticed in our survey of the existing Doctors is that they come from a wide variety of backgrounds, ranging from the comfortable family life of St Thérèse to the austere asceticism of St Jerome. Some had studied formally in the finest academic establishments of their age, like St Basil, others simply listened to the inspiration of the Scriptures and the liturgy of the Church, like St Anthony. Some were obviously pleasant people to meet, like St Francis de Sales, while others could be very difficult, like Cyril of Alexandria. Some advanced Christian theology in an obviously important way, like St Athanasius, while others simply preached to the simple people, like Peter Chrysologus. Some were well-known in their own times and afterwards, like St Gregory the Great, while others remained hidden in obscurity, like St Lawrence of Brindisi. What do they have in common? All were devoted to the Word of God, all eager to listen to the Holy Spirit, and to pass on to others what they had learned.

Blessed John Henry Newman

In September 2010, Pope Benedict XVI speculated publicly that Blessed John Henry Newman would fit the criteria laid down for a Doctorate. He certainly enjoyed the "Charism of Wisdom", with an acute mind and intellectual ability beyond most of us. His long ponderings on the Scriptures and the writings of the Church Fathers helped him to attain a "Mature Sapiental Synthesis": in particular, his thought on the relationship between faith and reason, religion and science, is peculiarly relevant today. Although we do not think of him as a spiritual writer, his letters of advice on prayer imply an "Authentic Spiritual Mastery". Certainly he was heroic in his "Christian Witness", for he gave up home, family and friends to follow where the light of truth led him, and so caused scandal or admiration among those who knew him. Despite the murmurings of those who pretended he was not fully Catholic, his affirmation by the Popes of his own time and afterwards shows that he was genuinely in touch with Catholic "Ecclesial Sources". And the criterion of "Wide Diffusion and Beneficial Influence" can hardly be questioned, since his writings have been read and appreciated in many languages, and have been an influence on great numbers of people in their journey towards faith.

It remains to be seen whether Newman will be canonised and subsequently declared a Doctor of the Church, or whether like Saints Peter Damian, Anselm, Albert, Peter Canisius and Robert Bellarmine, the granting of his Doctorate will automatically make him a Saint. We trust he will not have to wait 1,547 years like St Ephraem. There has probably been more international interest in declaring Newman a Doctor of the Church than for any of the thirty-three we have described, though he would be the first to hand the palm of greatest importance back to his role-models, Athanasius, Basil and Gregory.

Further Reading

Key texts

Spiritual Masters: The Fathers and Writers of the First Millennium (B 739)
Spiritual Masters: Medieval Fathers and Writers (B 740)

The Fathers of the Church (Do 780)

The Doctors of the Church

Augustine of Hippo (B 703)
Bernard of Clairvaux (B 735)
Anthony of Padua (B 679)
Thomas Aquinas (B 723)
Catherine of Siena (B 690)
Teresa of Avila (B 706)
John of the Cross (B 702)
Robert Bellarmine (B 728)
Francis de Sales (B 708)
Thérèse of Lisieux (B 204)

Blessed John Henry Newman

John Henry Newman (B 665)
Mind of Cardinal Newman, The (Do 738)
Newman Prayer Book (D 729)

Pope Benedict XVI
Spiritual Masters:
The Fathers & Writers of the
First Millennium

The ten catecheses in this richly illustrated volume take us back to the historical period immediately following the first Fathers of the Church. Each of the Spiritual Masters described by Pope Benedict left their own mark on the Church's culture and spirituality and helped in her growth.

ISBN: 978 1 86082 722 8

CTS Code: B 739

BENEDICT XVI
THE FATHERS & WRITERS
OF THE FIRST MILLENNIUM

The Spiritual Masters

CATHOLIC TRUTH SOCIETY

Pope Benedict XVI
Spiritual Masters:
The Medieval Fathers & Writers

In this richly illustrated volume, Pope Benedict examines the great Saints of the middle ages from St Odo, Abbot of Cluny, to St Peter Lombard the twelfth century theologian. With the Holy Father as our expert guide we delve into the great debates of scholastic and monastic theology meeting figures such as Hugh and Richard of Saint Victor, St Peter Damian and St Bernard of Clairvaux. An exploration of the theological meaning behind the Romanesque and Gothic Cathedral architecture of this time provides further depth.

ISBN: 978 1 86082 723 5

CTS Code: B 740

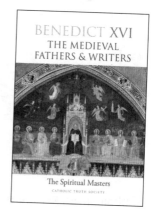